PIN-UP GIRLS

GRAYSCALE COLORING BOOK FOR ADULTS

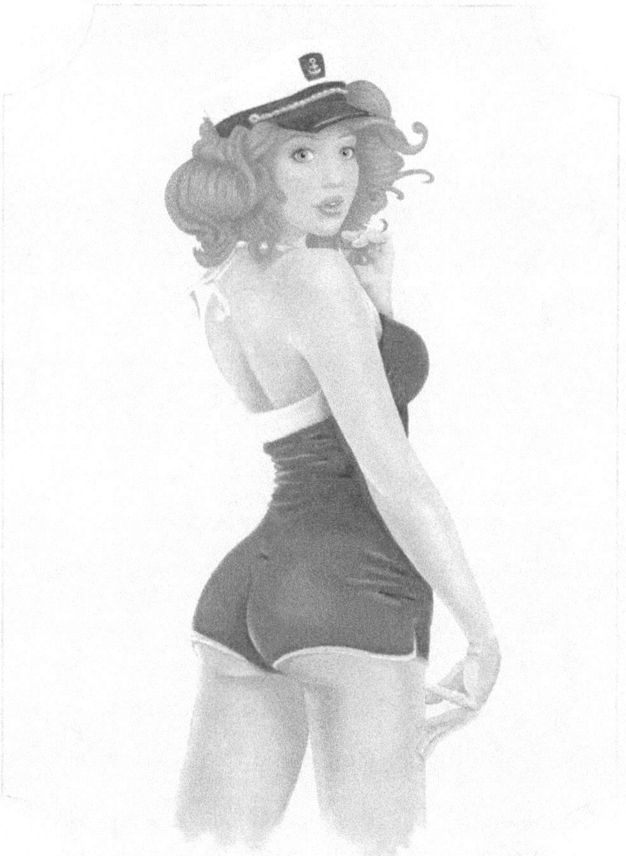

Majestic COLORING

www.MajesticColoring.com

ISBN: 978-1535184458

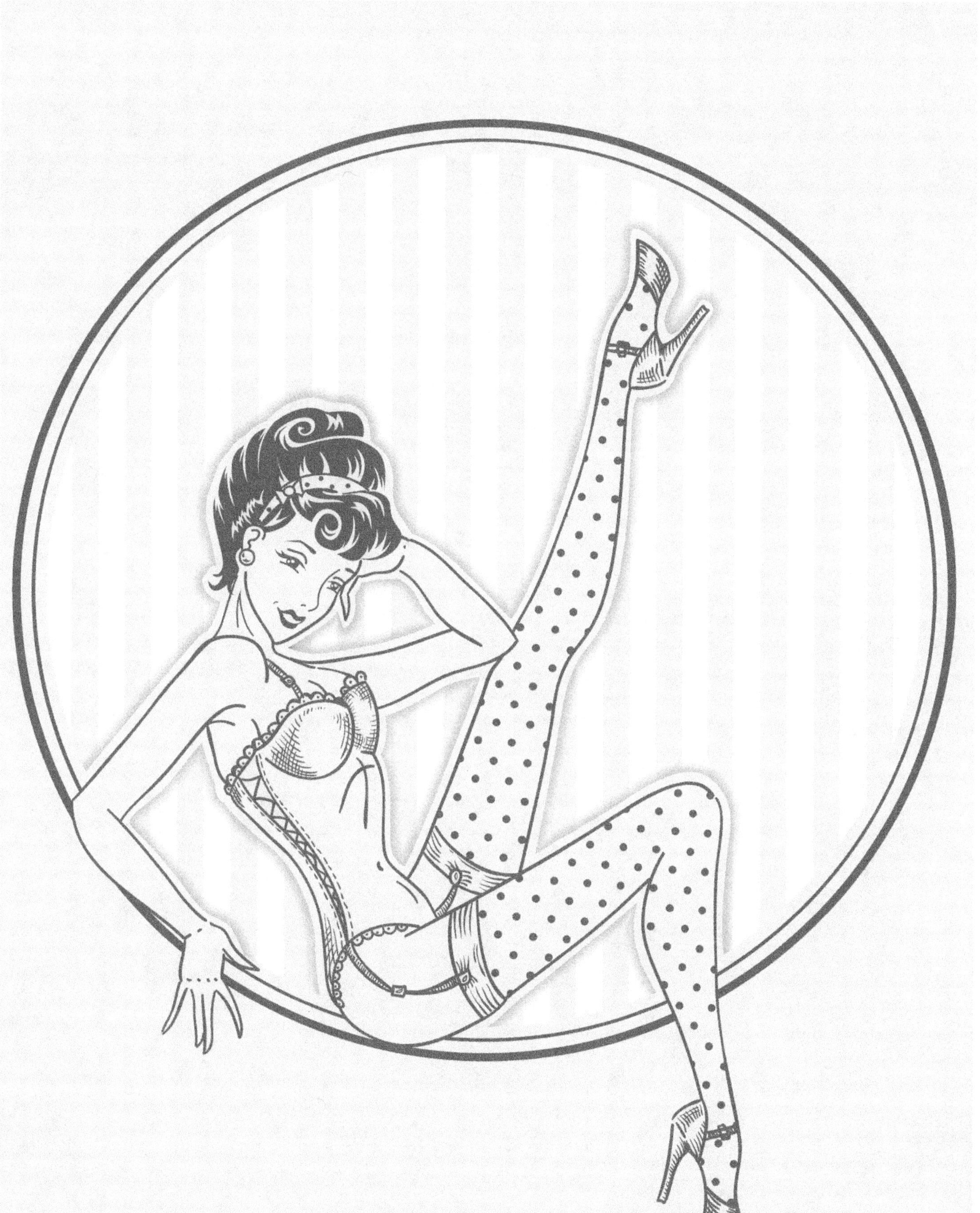

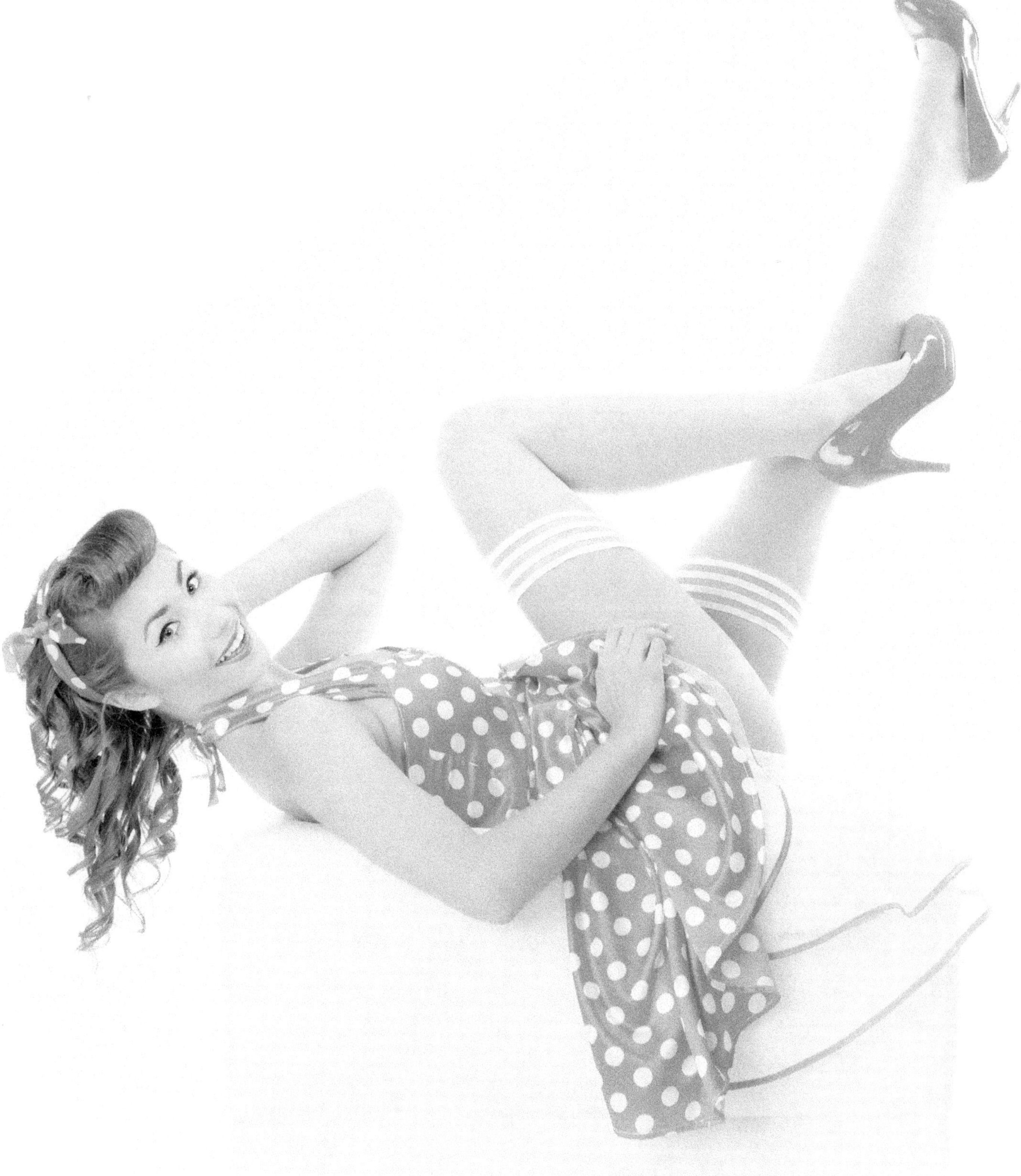

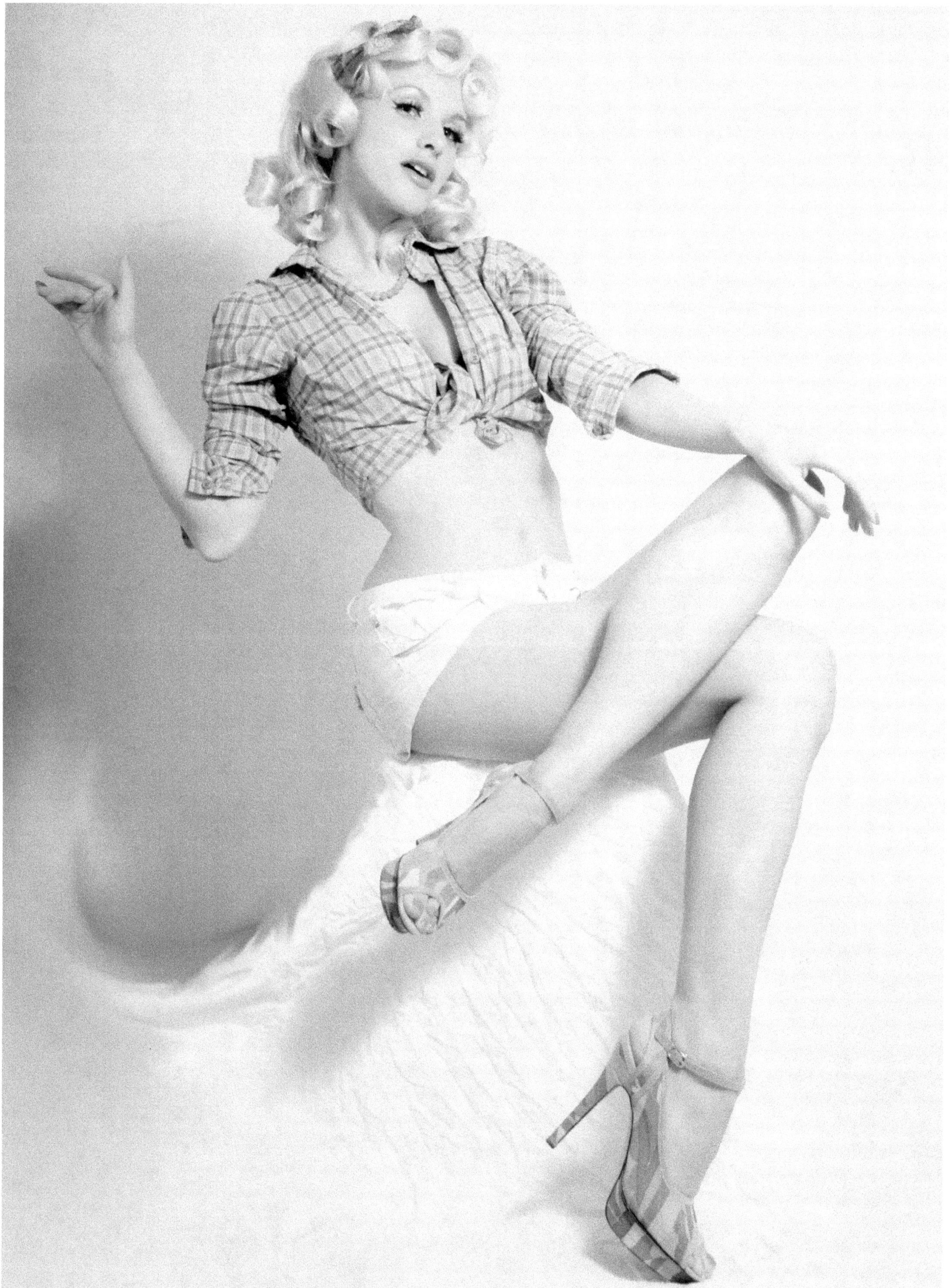

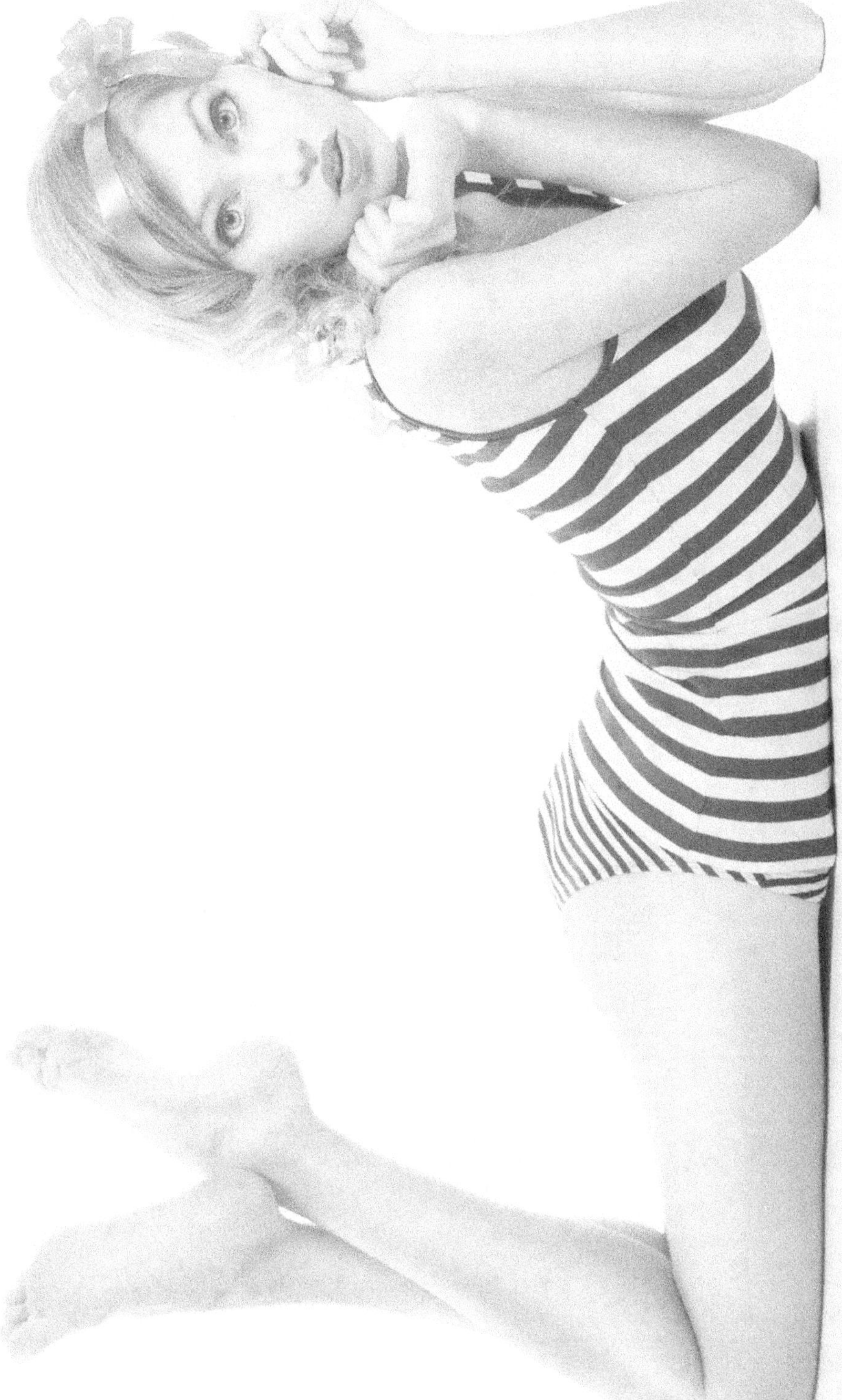

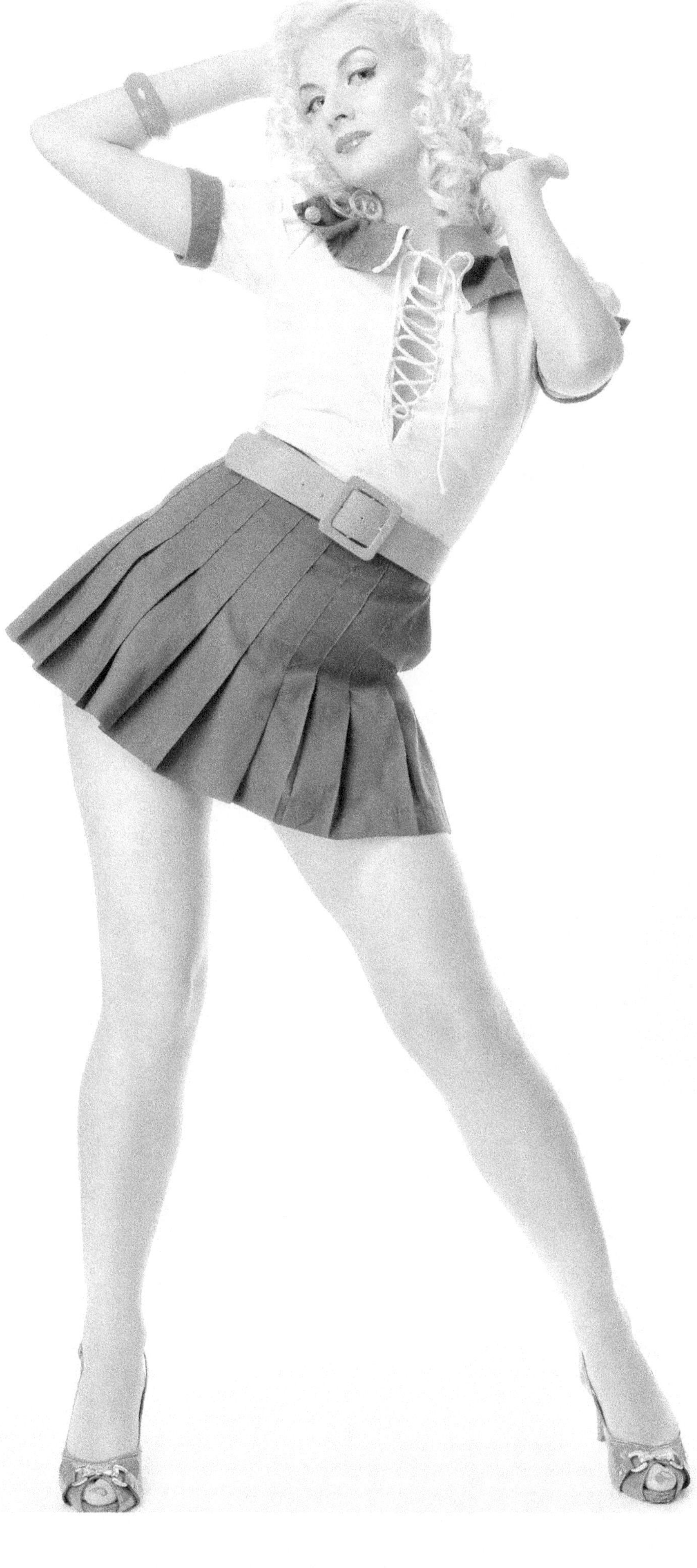

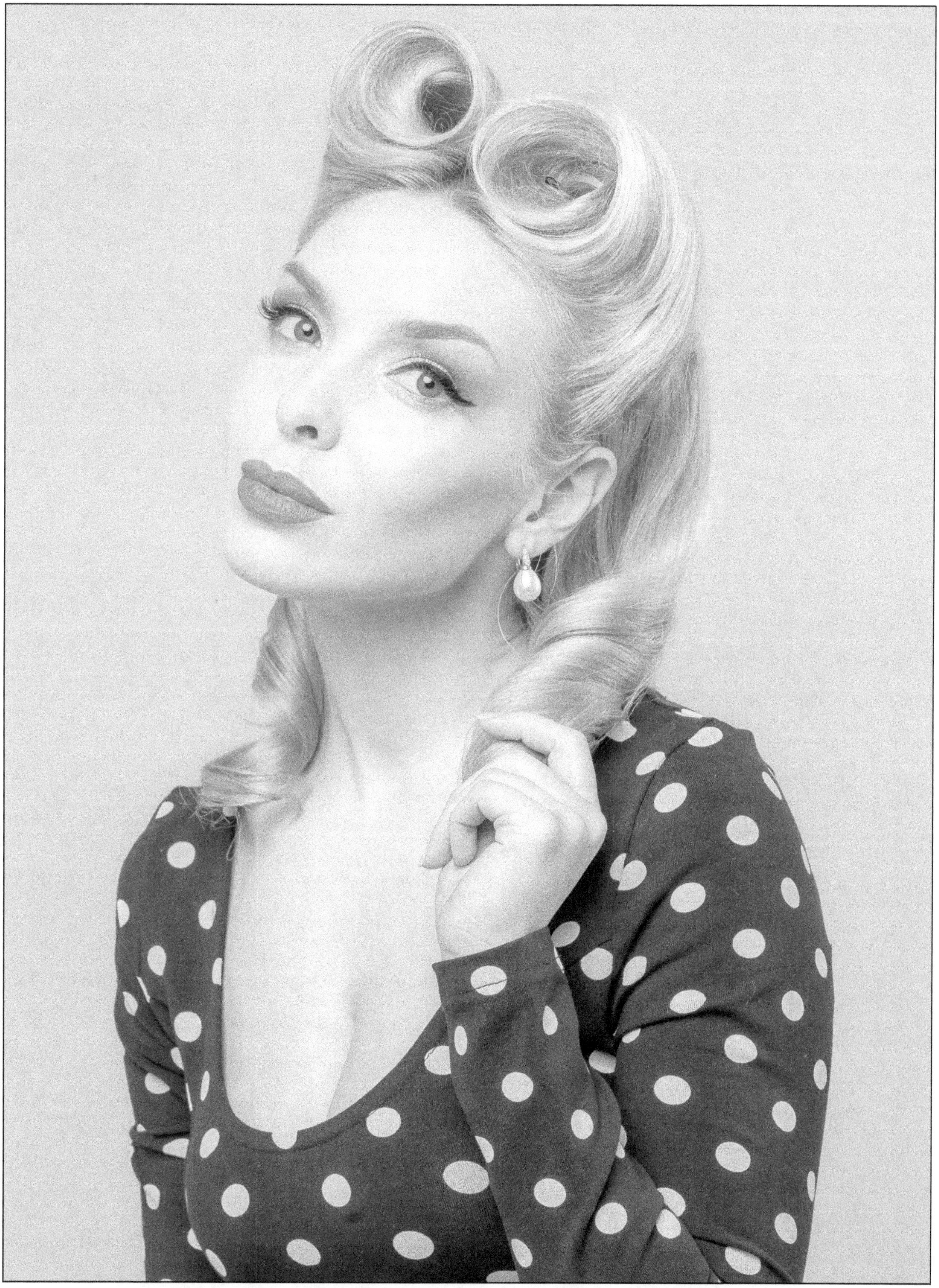

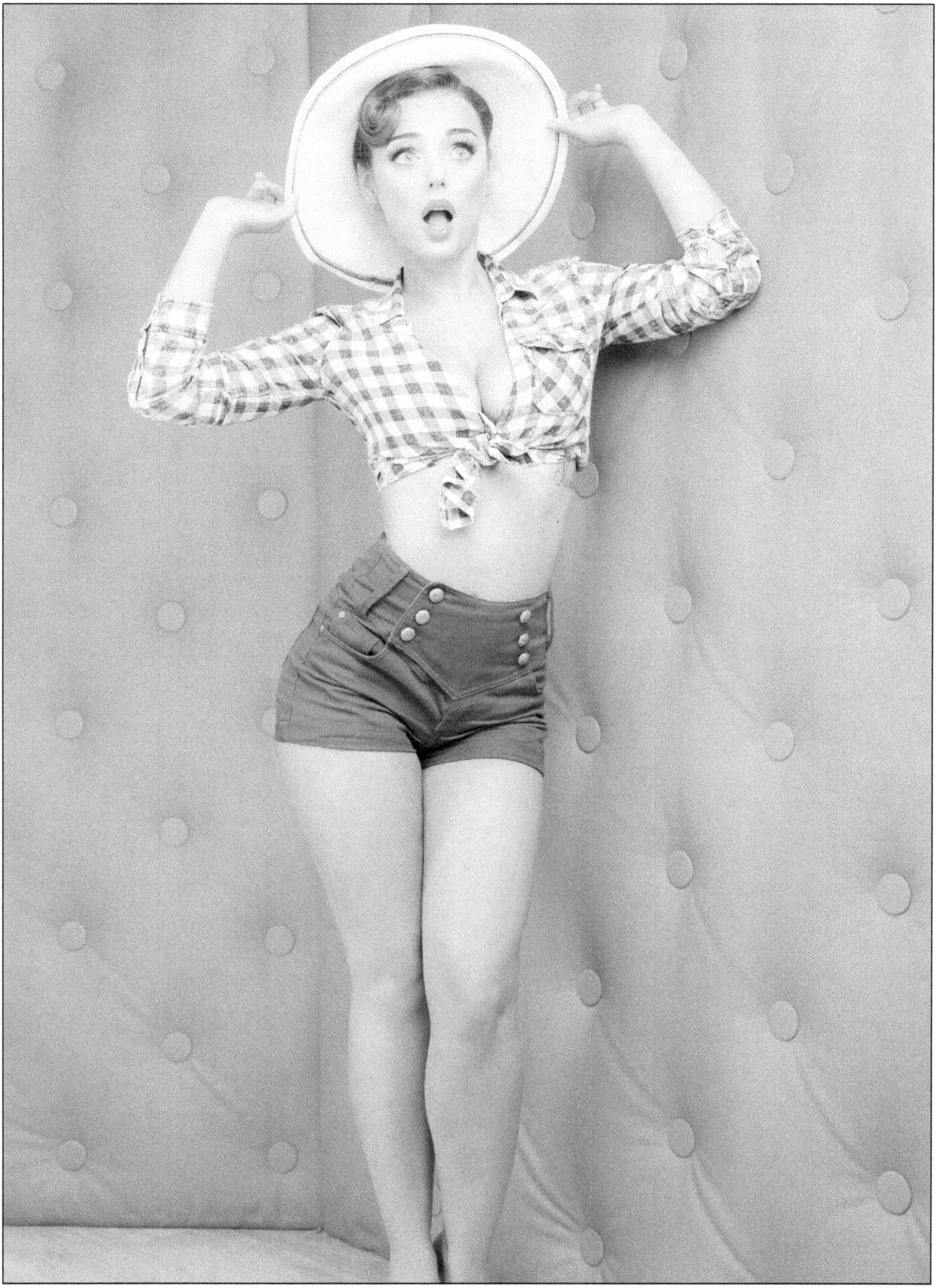

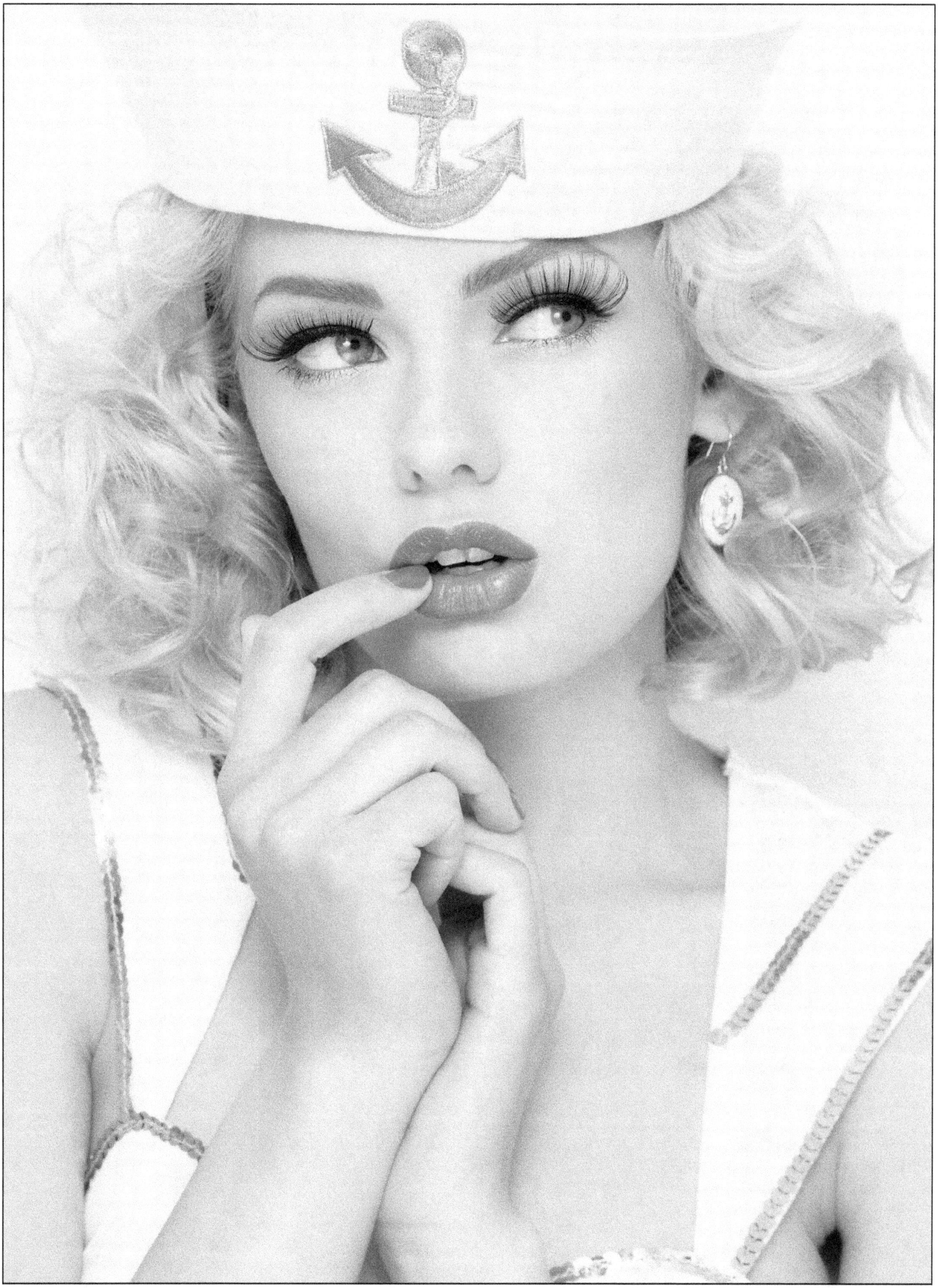

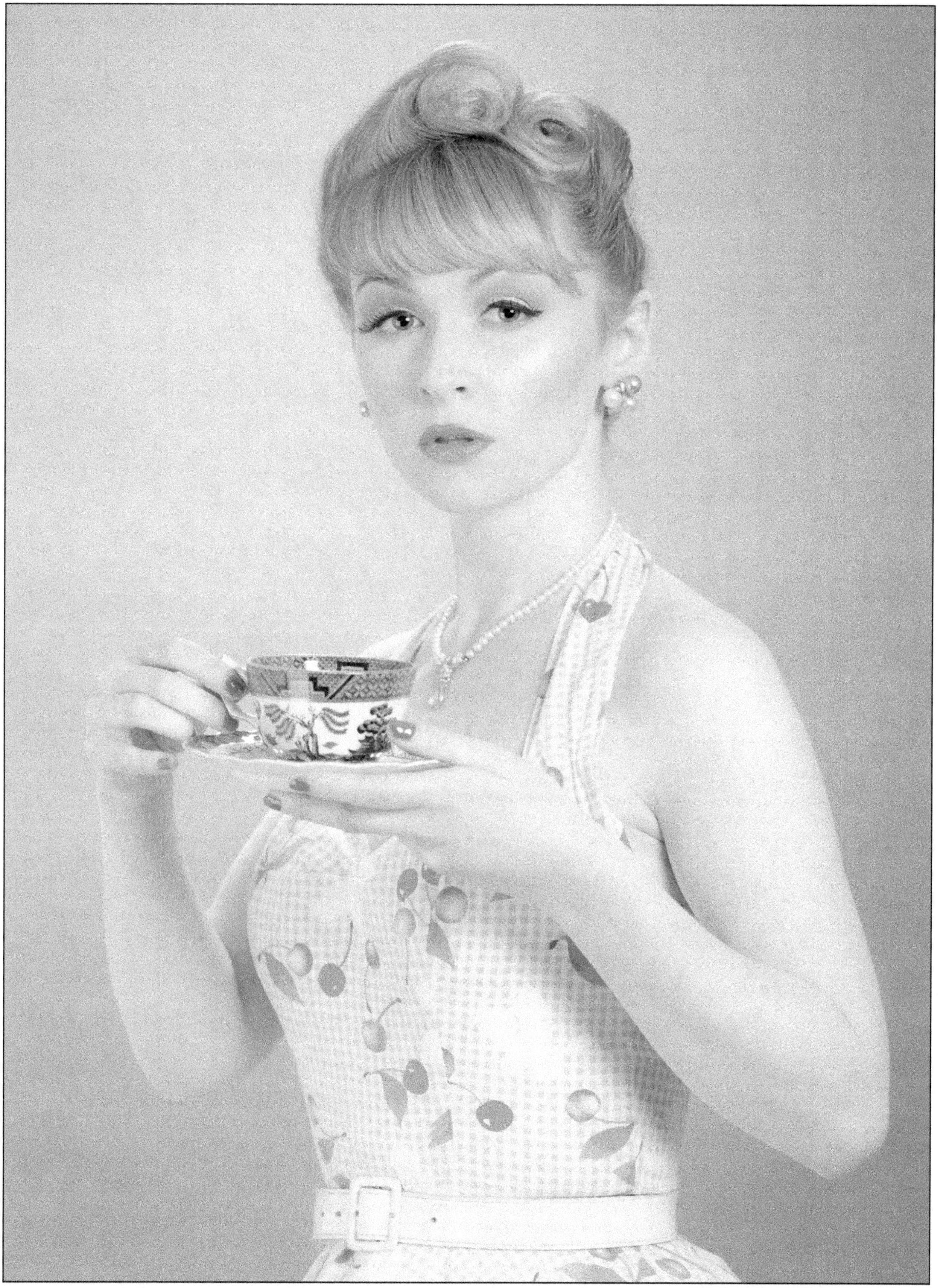

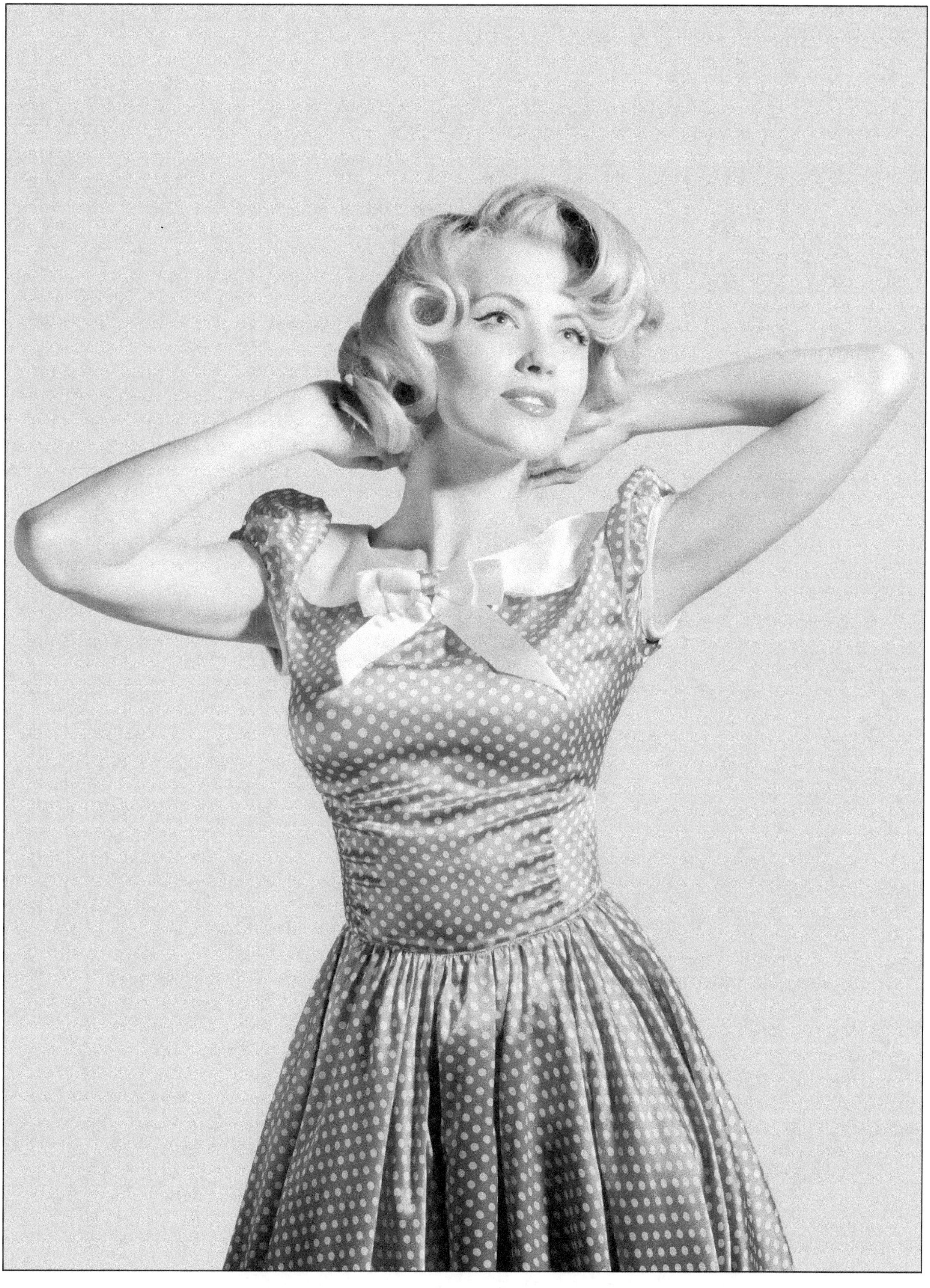

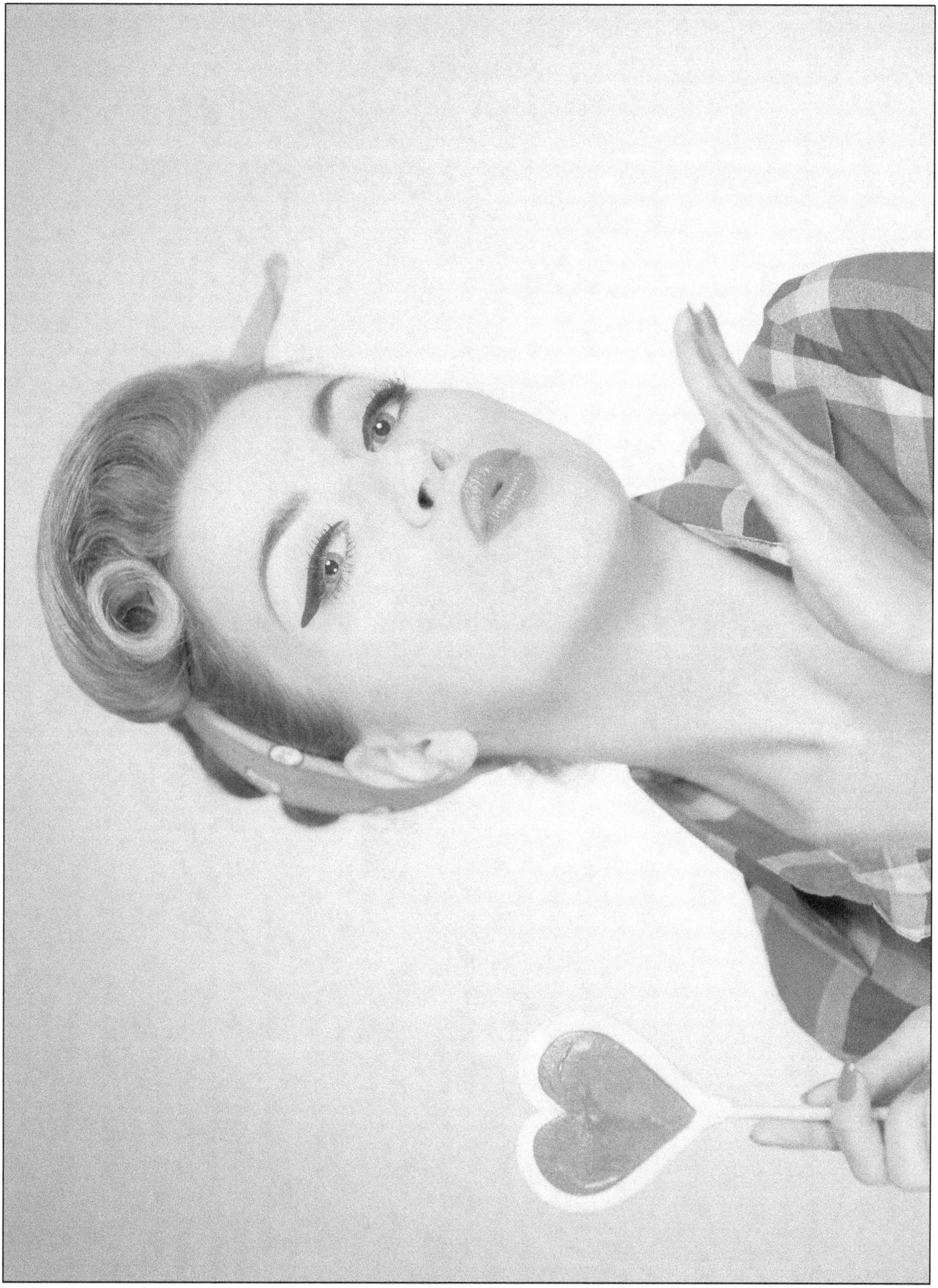

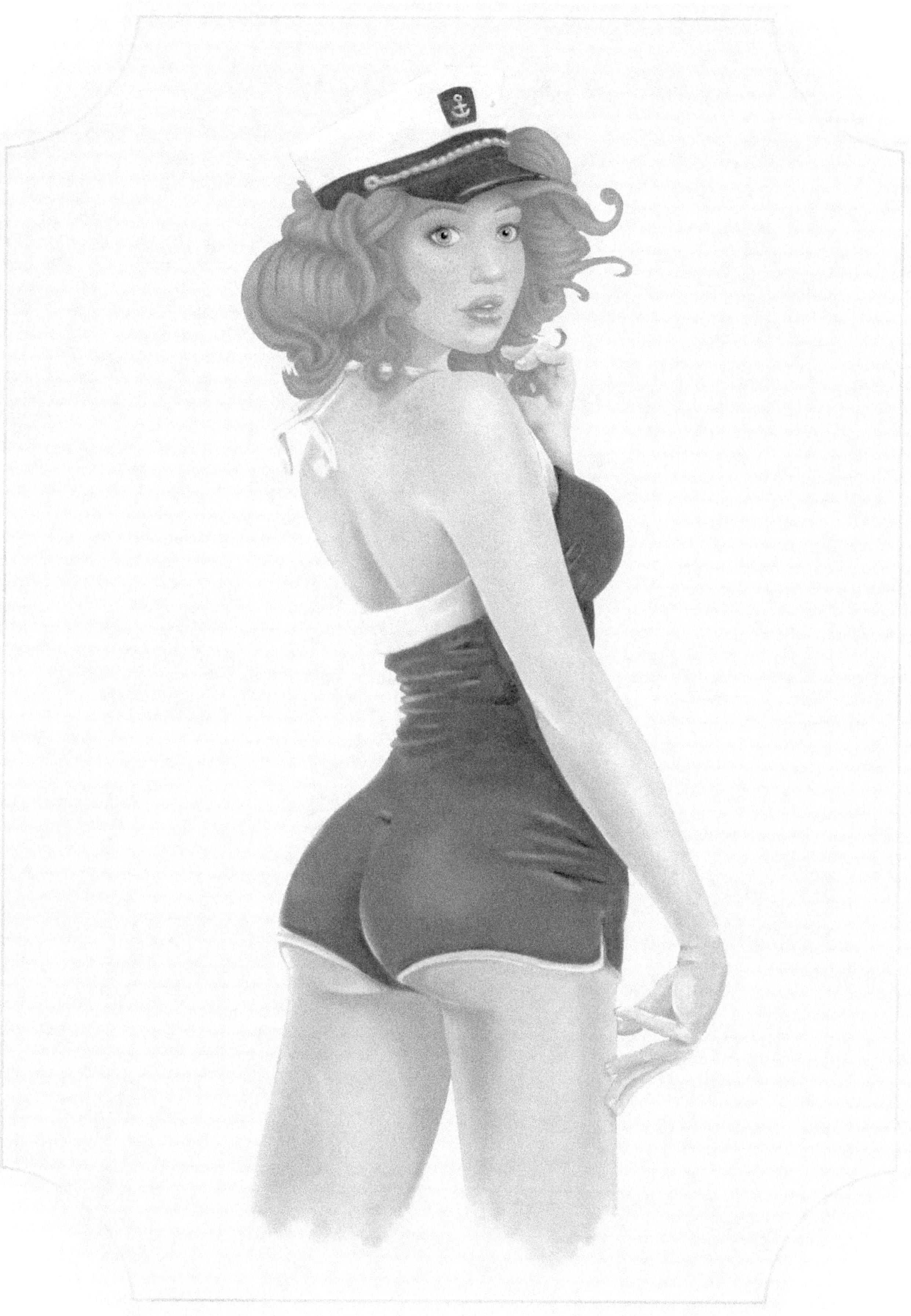

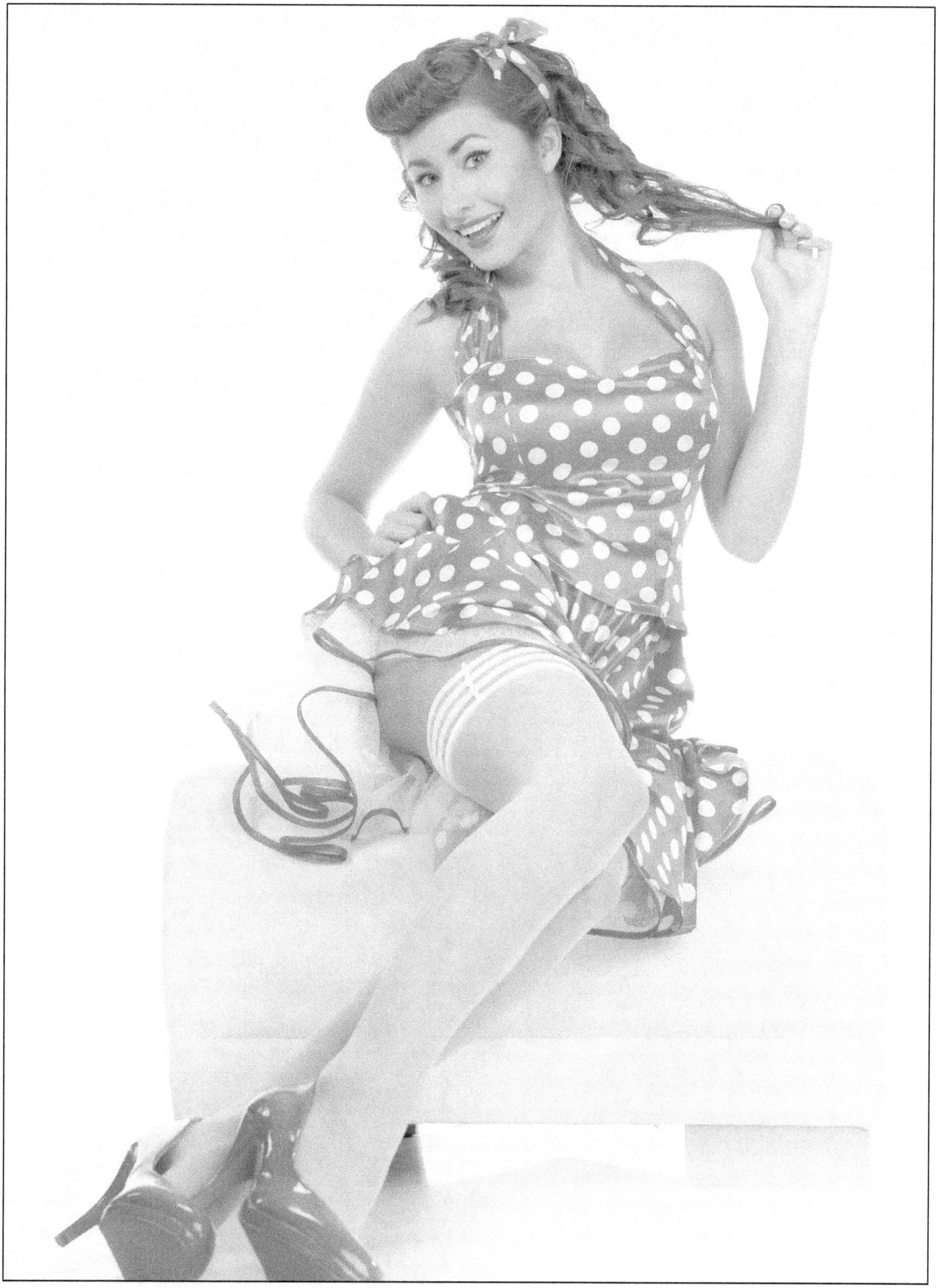

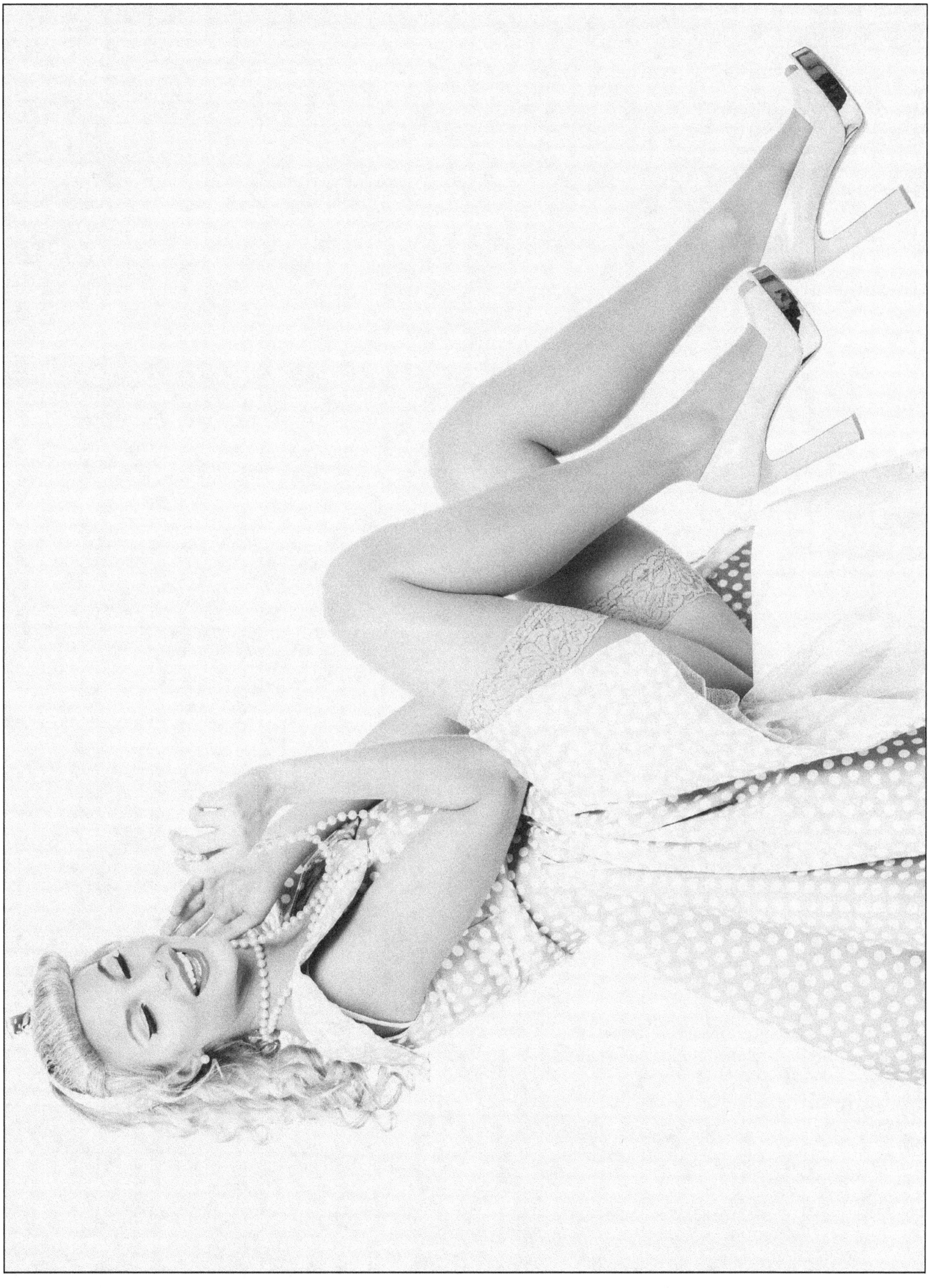

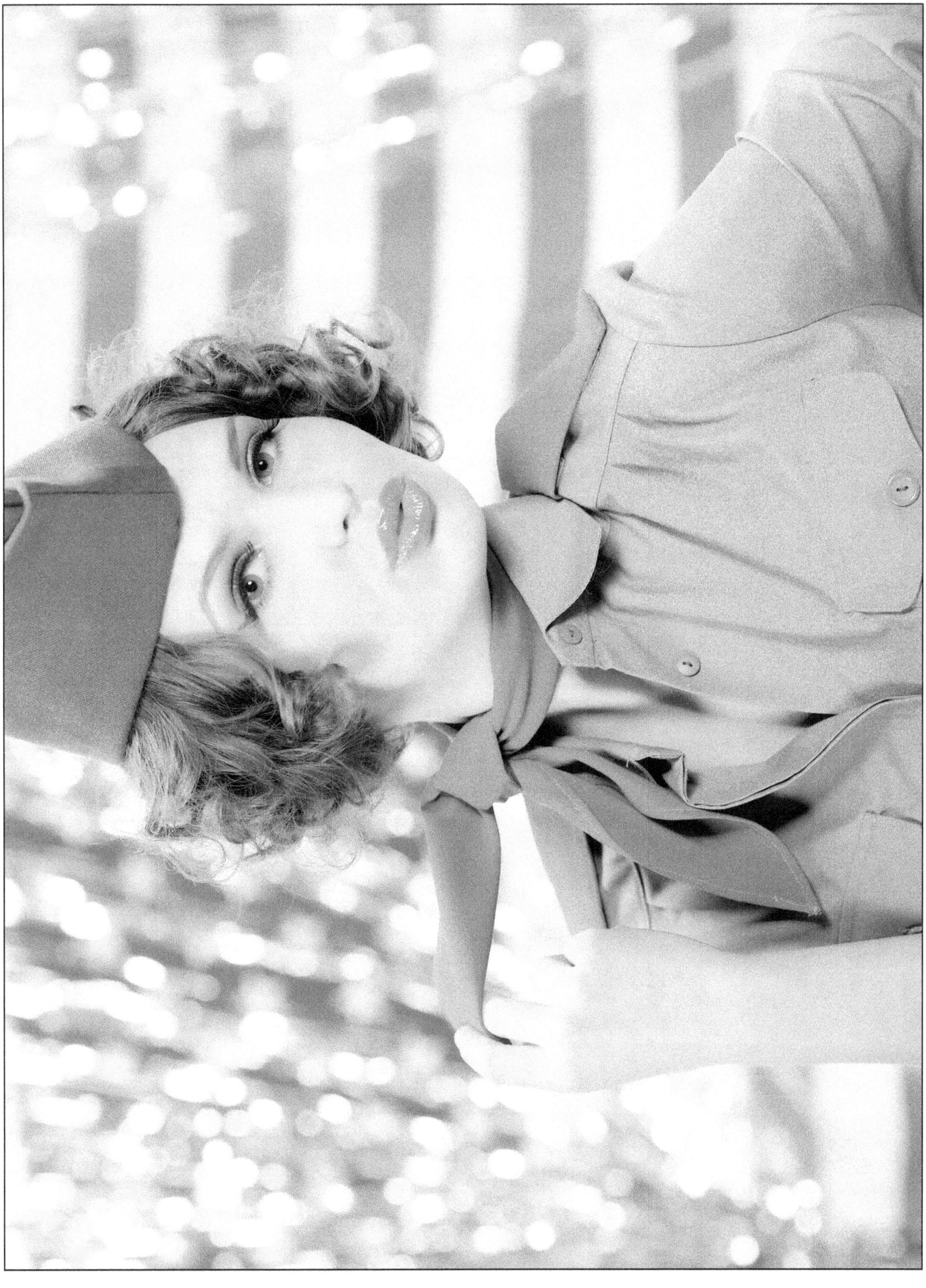

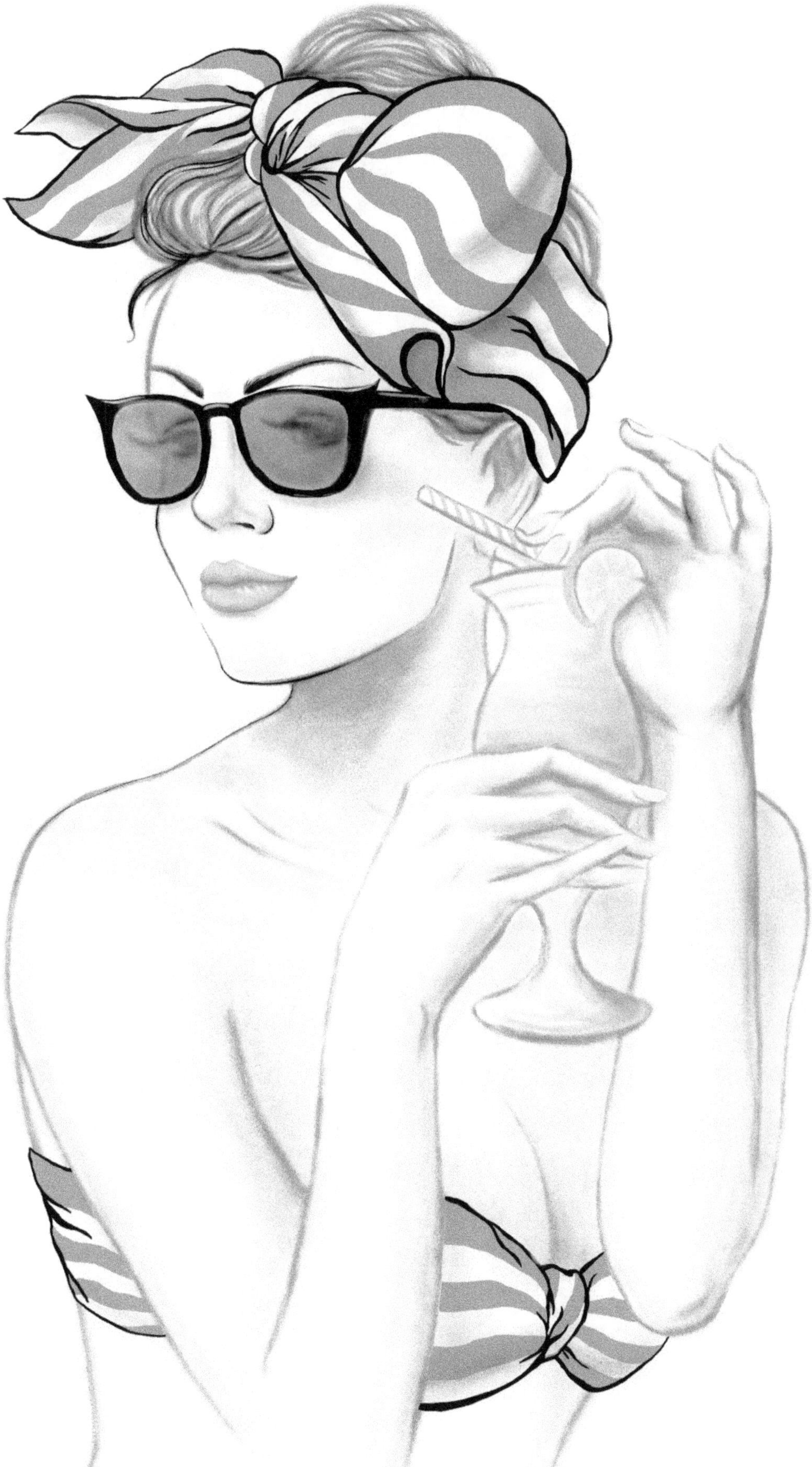

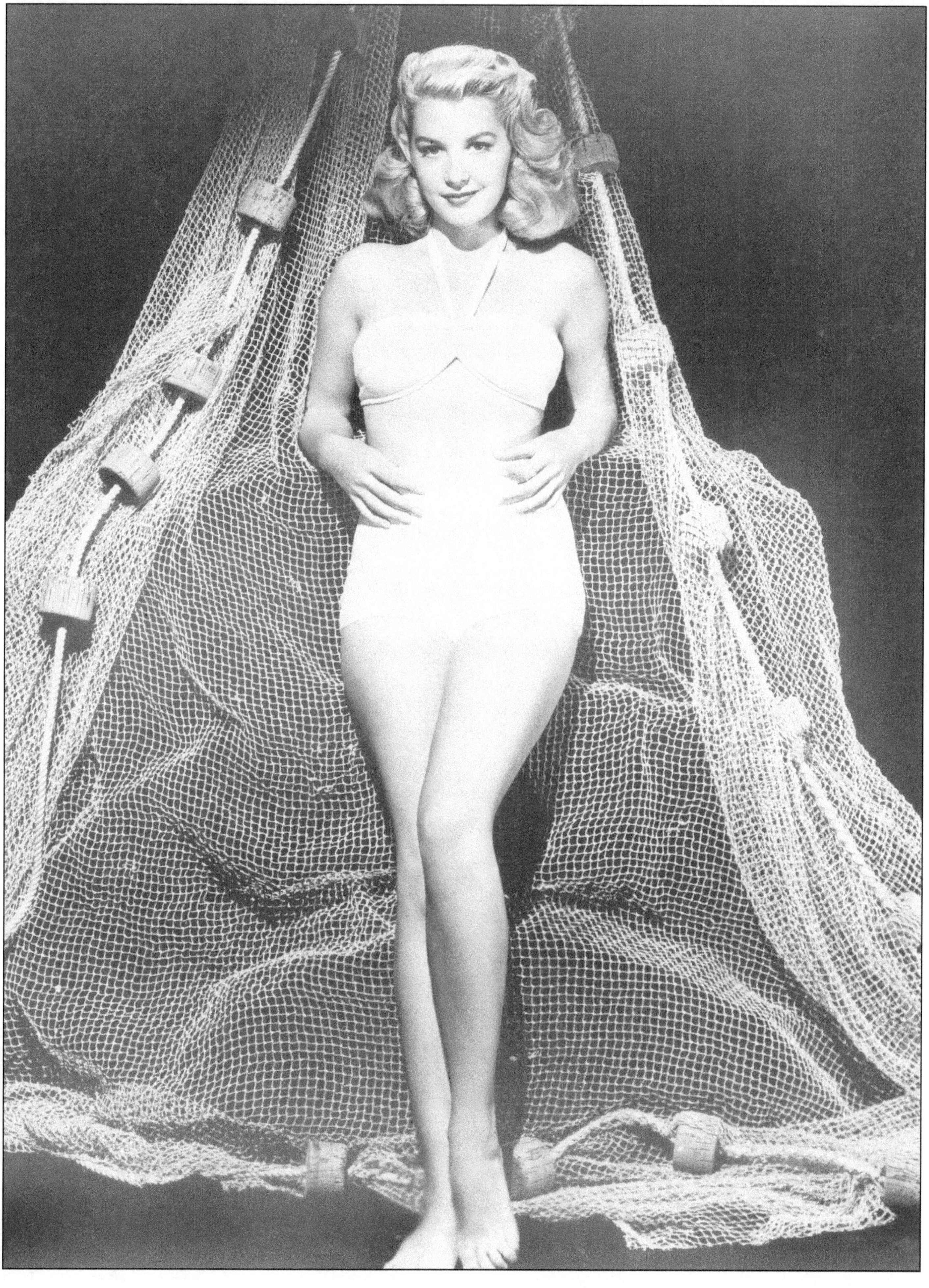

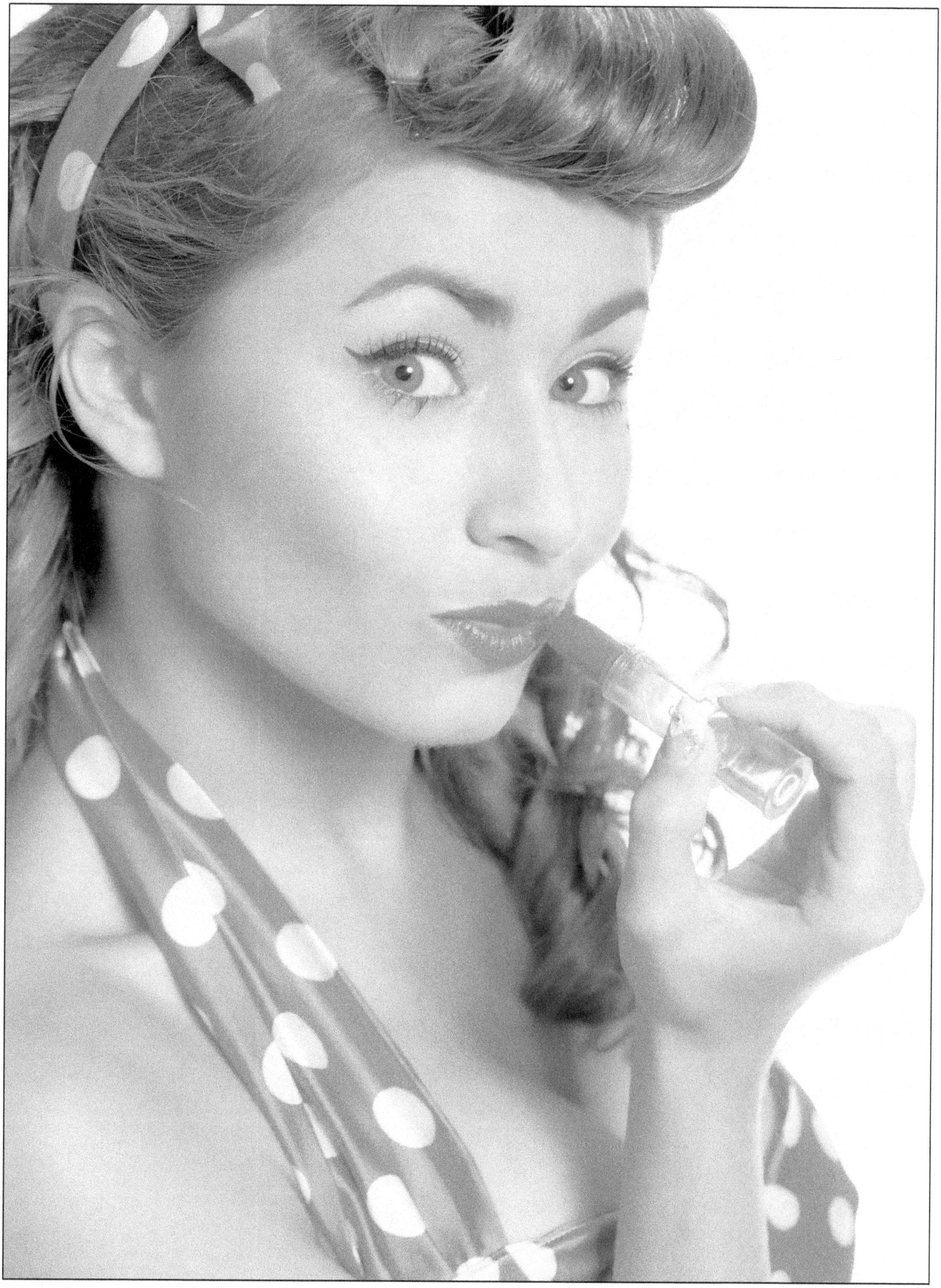

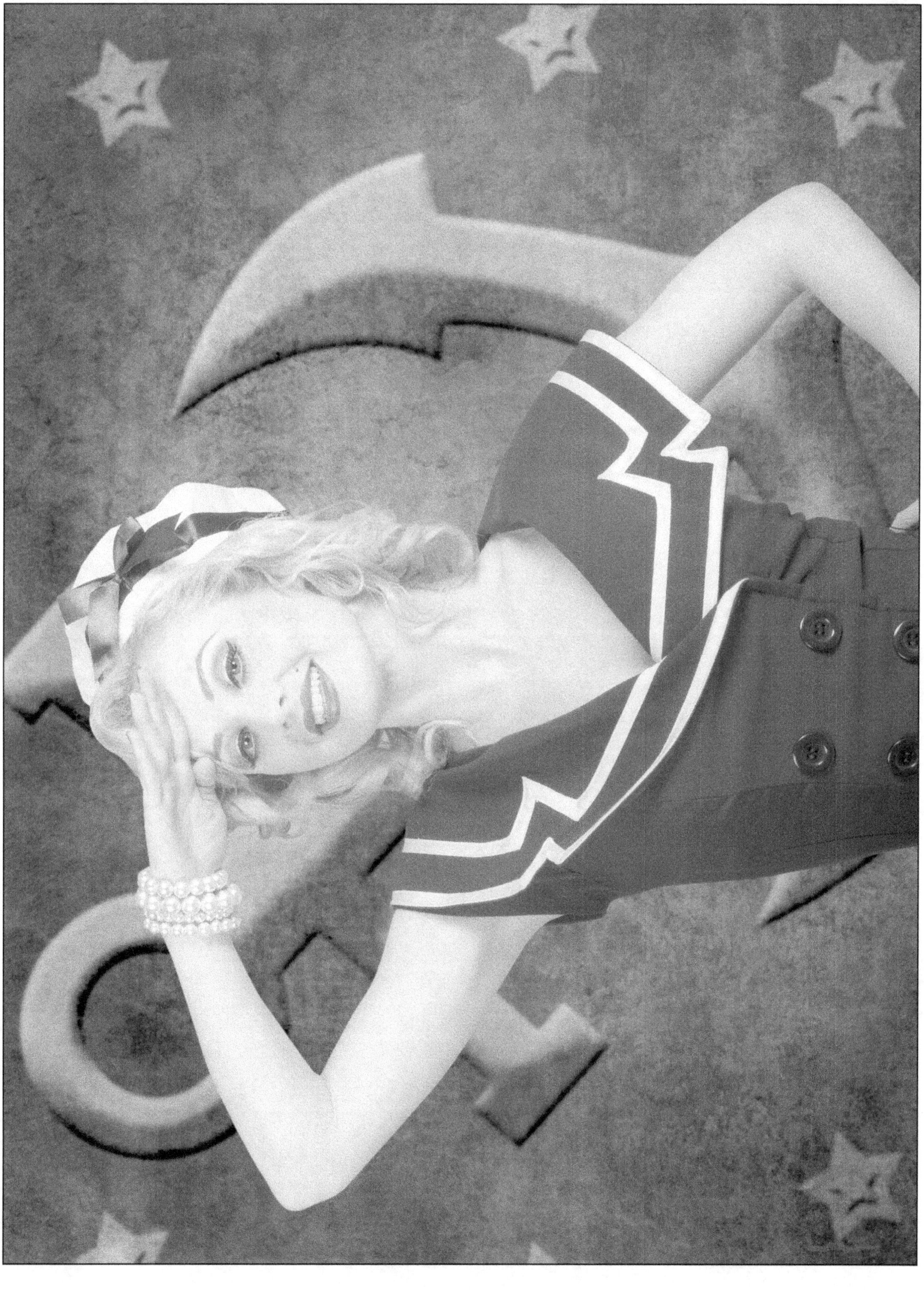

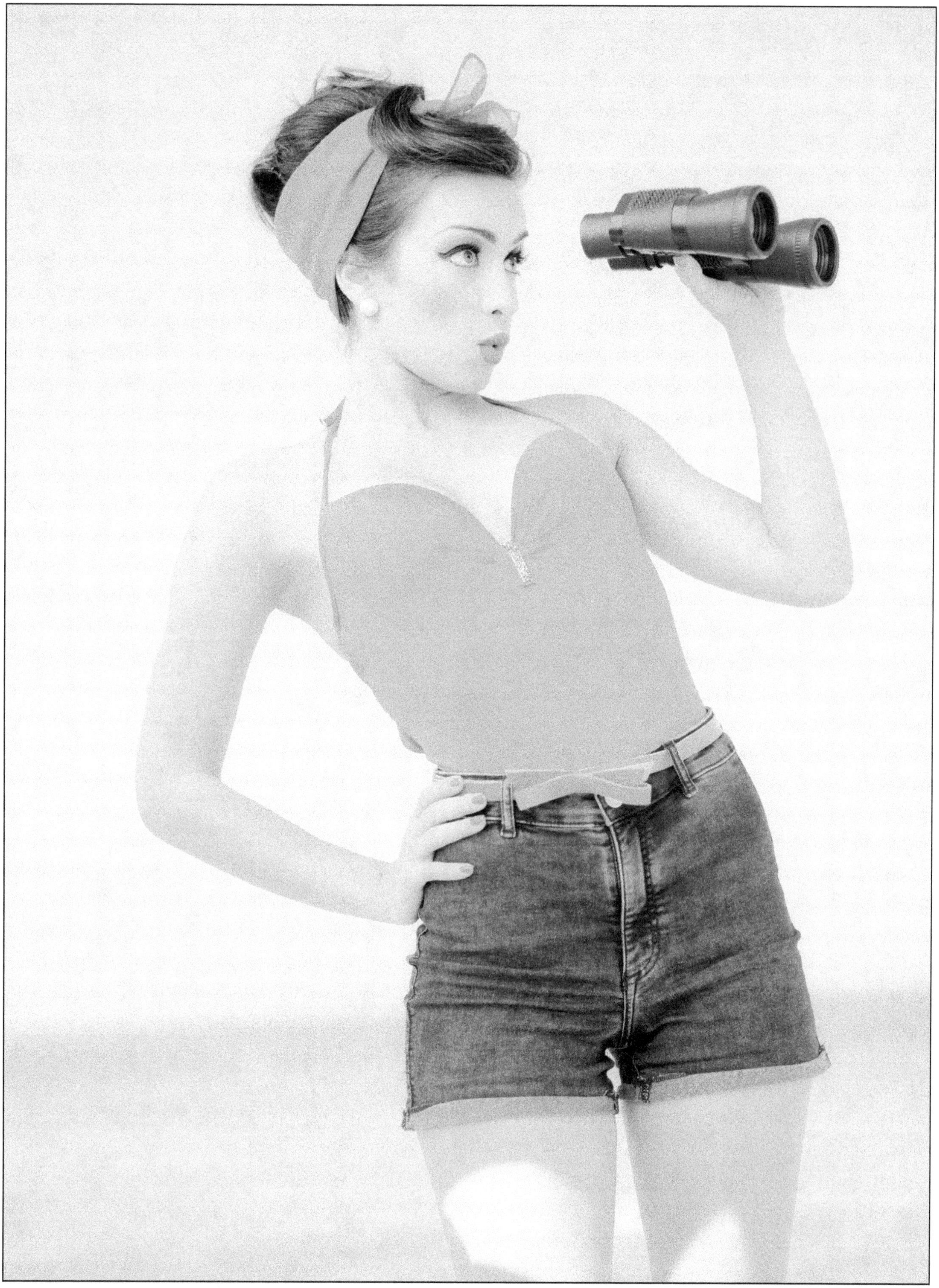

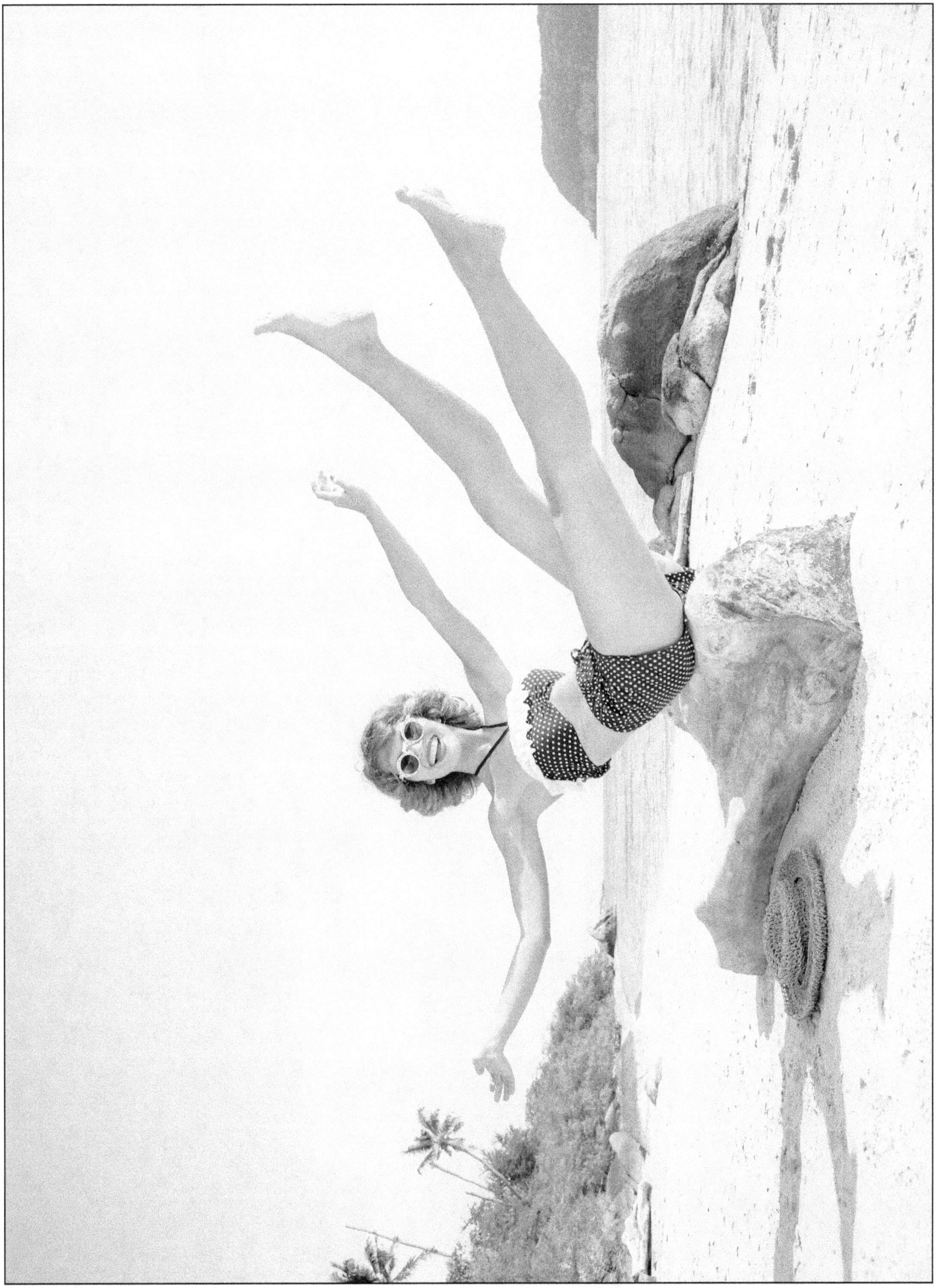

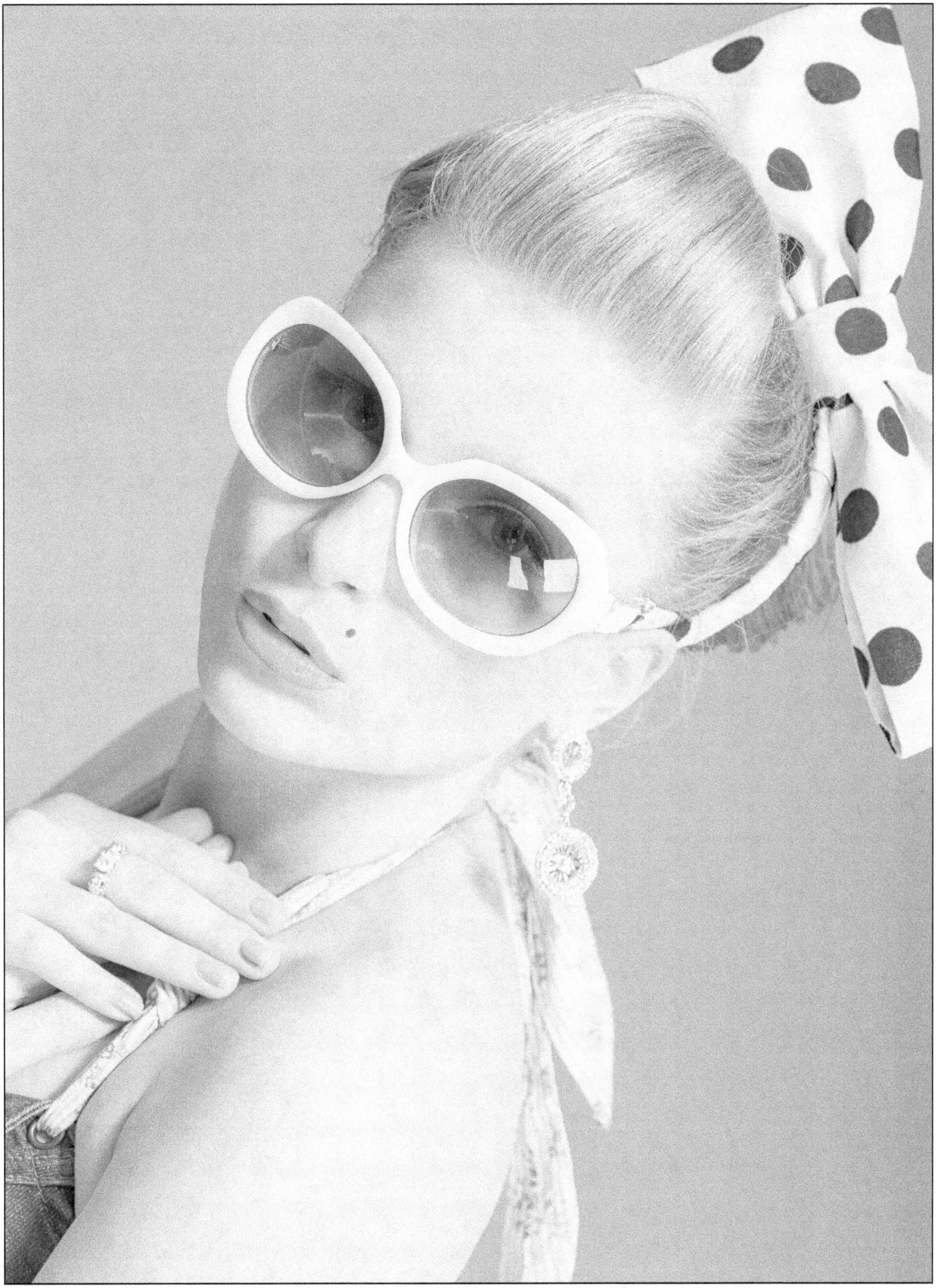

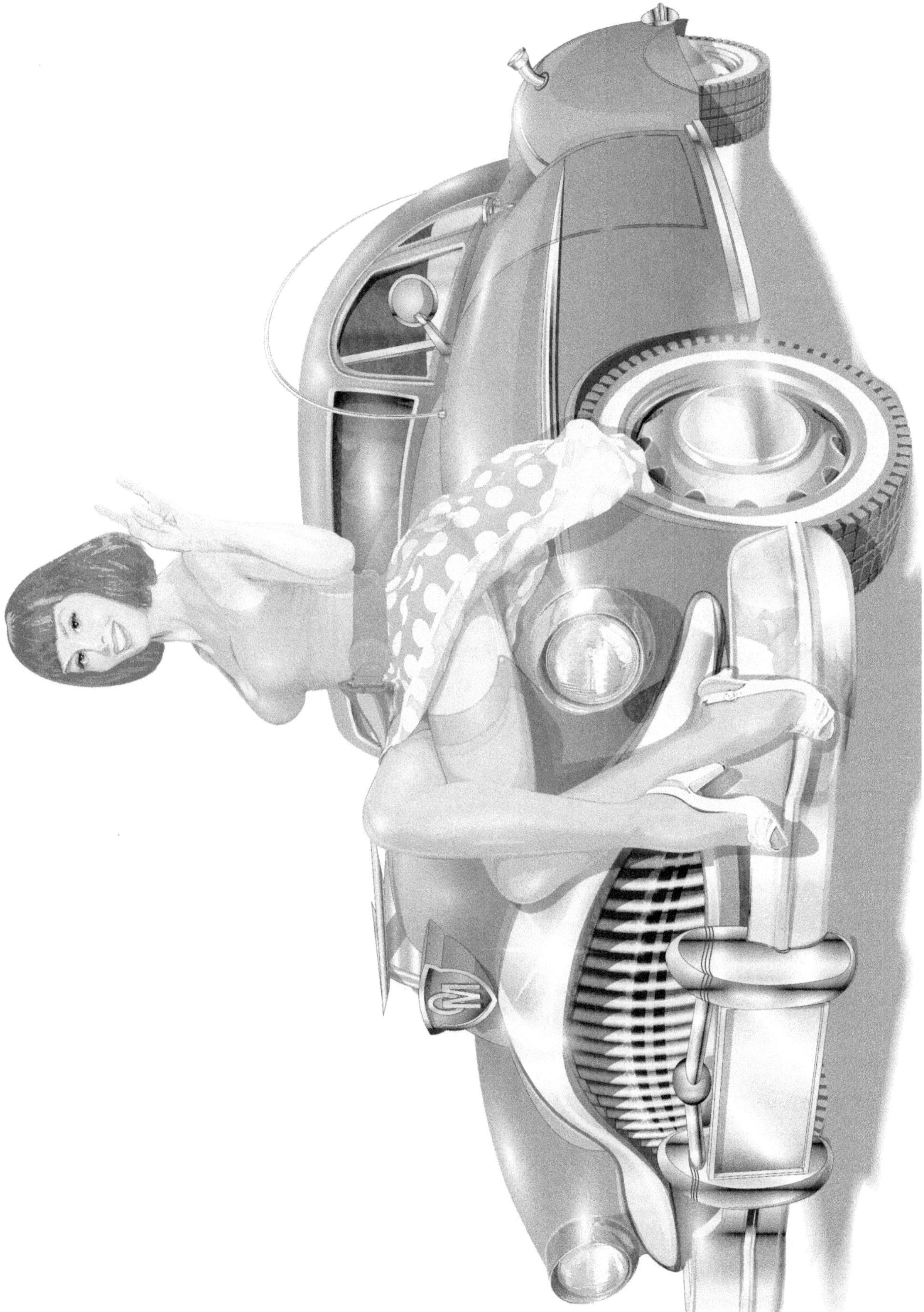

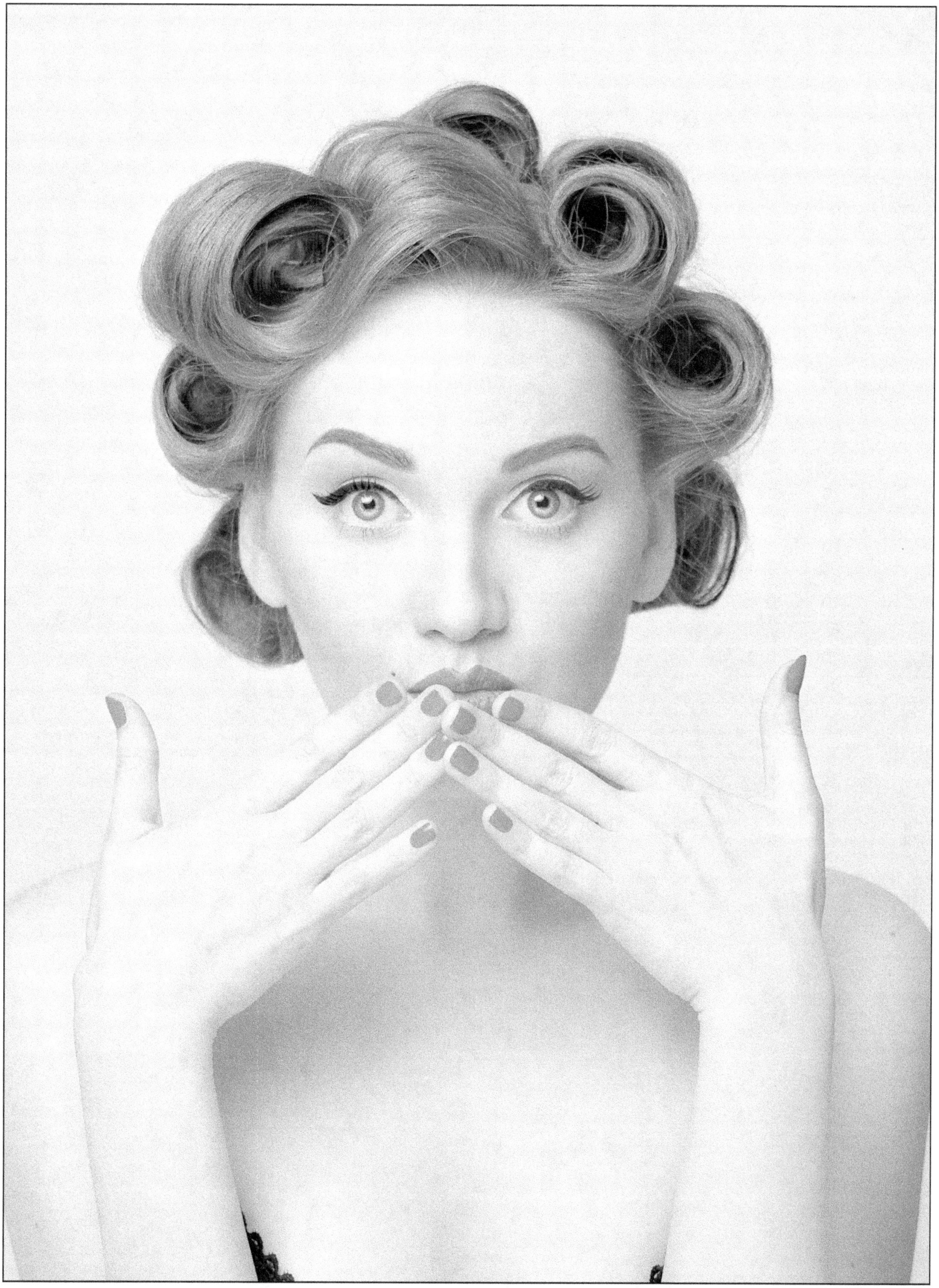

www.ingramcontent.com/pod-product-compliance
Lightning Source LLC
Chambersburg PA
CBHW080604190526
45169CB00007B/2878
9781535184458